SNOWFLAKE

by MIKE BARTLETT

Snowflake was first performed at the Old Fire Station, Oxford, on 5 December 2018.

SNOWFLAKE
by MIKE BARTLETT

CAST

ANDY	Elliot Levey
NATALIE	Racheal Ofori
MAYA	Ellen Robertson

COMPANY

Director	Clare Lizzimore
Assistant Director	Emily Collins
Designer	Jeremy Herbert
Lighting Designer	Jessica Hung Han Yun
Sound Designer	Steve Coe
Stage Manager	Jude Thorp
Assistant Stage Manager	Sophie Worters
Producer	Will Young
Producer for AOFS	Alexandra Coke

BIOGRAPHIES

ELLIOT LEVEY | ANDY

Theatre includes: *Mary Stuart* (Duke of York); *St Joan*, *Coriolanus* (Donmar Warehouse); *Much Ado About Nothing* (Wyndham's) *The Mighty Walzer* (Royal Exchange); *The Ruling Class* (Trafalgar Studios); *Danton's Death*, *The Habit of Art*, *All's Well That Ends Well*, *England People Very Nice*, *His Dark Materials*, *Henry IV Parts One and Two* (National Theatre); *Kafka's Dick* (Theatre Royal Bath); *Canvas* (Chichester Festival Theatre); *3 Sisters on Hope Street* (Hampstead); *Take Flight* (Menier Chocolate Factory); *How Much Is Your Iron?*, *Monkey!* (Young Vic); *On Ego*, *Love's Work*, *On Religion/Grace* (Soho); *Beasts and Beauties* (Bristol Old Vic); *Pidgin Macbeth*, *The Warp* (Ken Campbell Company); *The Tempest*, *Comedy of Errors* (RSC); *Tonight We Fly* (Trestle); *The Reckless are Dying Out* (Lyric Hammersmith); *Arabian Nights*, *The Soldier's Tale*, *If I Were Lifted Up* (Battersea Arts Centre).

Film includes: *The Chamber*, *Denial*, *The Lady in the Van*, *Florence Foster Jenkins*, *Spooks: The Greater Good*, *Philomena*, *Fallen*, *Murder on the Orient Express*, *The Queen*, *Filth and Wisdom*, *Supertex*, *Song of Songs*, *Book of John*.

Television includes: *Press*, *Watergate*, *Black Earth Rising*, *Grantchester*, *Silent Witness*, *Man Down*, *The Child in Time*, *A Midsummer Night's Dream*, *Ripper Street*, *Jamaica Inn*, *New Tricks*, *Touch of Cloth*, *Da Vinci's Demons*, *Parade's End*, *Hotel Babylon*, *Robin Hood*, *Monday Monday*, *Sex, The City and Me*, *Beau Brummell: This Charming Man*, *Amnesia*, *Lump in My Throat*, *Sirens*, *Jason and the Argonauts*, *Judas and Jesus*, *Casualty*, *EastEnders*, *Holby City*, *Fat Friends*, *Jesus*, *Lovejoy*.

RACHEAL OFORI | NATALIE

Theatre includes: *Blood Wedding* (Omnibus); *So Many Reasons* (Fuel); *Portrait* (Fuel/Camden People's Theatre); *Romeo and Juliet* (Garrick); *This Is Private Property* (Camden People's Theatre); *The Merchant of Venice* (Shakespeare's Globe); *A Midsummer Night's Dream* (Tooting Arts Club).

Film includes: *Guns Akimbo*, *Artemis Fowl*, *Ready Player One*.

Television includes: *Enterprice*, *Come Home*, *Carnage*, *Wizards vs. Aliens*.

ELLEN ROBERTSON | MAYA

Theatre includes: *Britney: The Show* (Battersea Arts Centre/Vault Festival/Edinburgh Fringe); *Britney in 'John'* (Edinburgh Fringe).

As Writer: *Nesting* (Watermill).

MIKE BARTLETT | WRITER

Plays for the theatre include: *Albion* (Almeida); *Wild* (Hampstead); *Game* (Almeida); *King Charles III* (Almeida/Wyndham's/Music Box, New York); *An Intervention* (Paines Plough/Watford); *Bull* (Sheffield Theatres/Off Broadway/ Young Vic); *Medea* (Headlong/Glasgow Citizens/Watford/Warwick); *Chariots of Fire* (Hampstead/Gielgud); *13* (National Theatre); *Decade* (co-writer Headlong); *Earthquakes in London* (Headlong/National Theatre); *Love,Love,Love* (Paines Plough/Plymouth Theatre Royal/Royal Court/Roundabout Theatre Company, New York); *Cock, Contractions, My Child* (Royal Court); *Artefacts* (Bush/Nabokov).

As Director: *Medea* (Headlong/Glasgow Citizens/Watford/Warwick); *Honest* (Theatre Royal Northampton).

Television includes: *Press* (BBC); *Trauma* (ITV); *King Charles III* (Drama Republic/ BBC); *Doctor Foster* (Drama Republic/BBC); *The Town* (Big Talk Productions).

CLARE LIZZIMORE | DIRECTOR

Directing includes: *Bull* by Mike Bartlett (Crucible Studio, Sheffield/59E59, New York/Young Vic, London); *One Day When We Were Young* by Nick Payne (Paines Plough/Sheffield Theatres/Shoreditch Town Hall); *Lay Down Your Cross* by Nick Payne, *On the Rocks* by Amy Rosenthal (Hampstead); *Pieces of Vincent* by David Watson (Arcola); *Faces in the Crowd* by Leo Butler, *The Mother, Fear and Misery, War and Peace* by Mark Ravenhill (Royal Court); *Jonah and Otto* by Robert Holman (Royal Exchange, Manchester); *Tom Fool* by Franz Xaver Kroetz (Citizens, Glasgow/Bush) and *The Most Humane Way to Kill a Lobster* by Duncan Macmillan (Theatre503).

As Writer: *Animal* (Atlantic Theatre, New York and Studio Theatre, Washington D.C) and *Mint* (Royal Court). Clare is also under commission with The Royal Court Theatre and Almeida Theatre.

Radio includes: *The Rage* and *Missing in Action* (both BBC Radio 4).

Awards include: Olivier Award for Outstanding Achievement In An Affiliate Theatre, Channel 4 Theatre Directors Award (formerly the RTYDS Award), and the Arts Foundation Theatre Directing Fellowship. Clare has been resident director at Citizens Theatre, Glasgow and a staff director at the National Theatre.

JEREMY HERBERT | DESIGNER

Jeremy is a multimedia artist and stage designer.

He most recently designed *Stories* (National Theatre); *The Wind* (Royal Ballet); *Blue Orange, Why It's Kicking Off Everywhere* (with journalist Paul Mason) at the Young Vic; the operas *La Bianca Notte* (Hamburg Staatsoper) and *Rodelinda* (ENO/Bolshoi).

His most recent art installations have been Underbelly at Frieze, and Safe House at the Young Vic. He created the stage set for PJ Harvey's Hope 6 Demolition Project world tour.

JESSICA HUNG HAN YUN | LIGHTING DESIGNER

Lighting design credits include: *Hive City Legacy* (Hot Brown Honey/ Roundhouse); *The Party's Over* (Lakeside Theatre Nottingham); *Forgotten* (Arcola); *Becoming Shades* (Vaults festival); *Nine Foot Nine* (Bunker); *The Human Voice* (Gate); *One* (Bert & Nasi international tour); *A Pupil* (Park); *Cuckoo* (Soho).

The Old Fire Station has been a popular Oxford venue for many years (since way before Mike Bartlett directed a show here as a teenager). But since it was refurbished and reopened in 2011, it has become something extra special.

In just seven years, we have created a popular thriving multi-form arts centre presenting work by the best small-scale touring companies as well as local talent, organising festivals such as Offbeat (our own mini Edinburgh Fringe) and mounting a varied programme of exhibitions in the gallery and elsewhere. We host around twenty regular dance classes every week and have a gorgeous shop selling contemporary craft and feel-good gifts. We also support artists by offering studio space and help with creative and technical processes and in marketing, fundraising, selling and networking. We have gradually developed a coherent and distinctive artistic offer to the public as a receiving house, a curator and a producer. Through close partnership working, we have become a hub for artists of all disciplines to test ideas, make and showcase great work.

But what makes us extra special is that we share our building with the homelessness charity Crisis. Through this partnership, we've developed a nationally recognised model of social inclusion – enabling people facing tough times to see shows, volunteer, train, get paid work, create art and help run the arts centre.

And we think deeply about what we are doing and what impact we are having – mainly by asking people to tell us stories about what change has happened for them and how.

Our spaces are intimate, inspiring, professional and accessible to all. The public comes to drink coffee, buy art, attend classes and watch shows. Homeless people come to learn, gain skills and get support. Artists come to rehearse, create and showcase. They all come through the same door and find themselves sharing space and interests. We focus on good quality relationships, encouraging creativity and risk-taking, and offering a truly inclusive public space.

Oxford is globally renowned for stunning heritage and outstanding research. But it's also a place of disadvantage and inequality.

Oxford needs the Old Fire Station because it is about openness, inclusion, looking forward and different thinking. The Old Fire Station acts as a bridge between sectors, organisations and people.

WHAT WE DO

Presenting new work across art forms – we want our reputation to be good quality art aimed at adults which takes a risk, asks questions and entertains. We want our audiences to have fun and be open to new ideas and different people.

Supporting artists – we support early to mid-career artists from all disciplines with advice, networks and promotion to help them become more successful.

Including people facing tough times – we share our building with the homelessness charity, Crisis. Through this partnership, we offer people who are homeless space to define themselves and choose their own labels by including them in the running of the centre – as audience, participants, volunteers and co-creators. We look for ways of including those who are socially isolated and disadvantaged. This improves the quality of what we do, helps develop networks, builds resilience and leads to more stable lives.

We do this, with Crisis, by offering a public space which is shared by very different people and helps to break down barriers and promote solidarity in Oxford.

Back in 2015, Jonny Donahoe agreed to write our first ever Christmas show for grown-ups which resulted in *30 Christmases* in December 2016. He followed up the following year by writing *Working Christmas* for us with James Rowland. And in 2018 he introduced us to his old friend, Mike Bartlett. So, thank you, Jonny, for enabling us to make this special offer for grown-ups at Christmas and to Will Young for co-producing and holding our hands so firmly, thank you, Mike, for writing such a timely witty play and thank you to Clare Lizzimore, the cast and creative team for turning it into this wonderful premiere.

Snowflake is about Britain in 2018 but it is also about the enduring truth that it is possible to find meaning and happiness if we commit ourselves to what matters most – how we get on together. That's why it is the perfect show for the Old Fire Station

We need friends to support us so, if you'd like to know more about what happens at the Old Fire Station, just get in touch.

oldfirestation.org.uk

Supporters of *Snowflake*

Andrew Lloyd Webber Foundation; Andrew Fairweather-Tall;
Chiltern insurance Group; David & Liz Coke; Laura Jones; Michael
Mossop; New Diorama Theatre; Paul Clayton; Sir Nicholas Hytner;
Stephen Waley-Cohen; The Roundton Trust; Unity Theatre Trust;
Will Young; Windich Legal; and all of our supporters who wish to
remain anonymous.

Special thanks to Arts Council England, Oxford City Council and
Novel Entertainment.

SNOWFLAKE

Mike Bartlett

Acknowledgements

Thank you to the following, without whom this play would not exist:

Jonny Donahoe, Clare Lizzimore, Jeremy Herbert, Jeremy Spafford, Will Young.

M.B.

To Audrey

Characters

ANDY
NATALIE
MAYA

(/) *means the next speech begins at that point.*
(–) *means the next line interrupts.*
(…) *at the end of a speech means it trails off. On its own it indicates a pressure, expectation or desire to speak.*

A line with no full stop at the end indicates that the next speech follows on immediately.

A speech with no written dialogue indicates a character deliberately remaining silent.

Dialogue in brackets indicates the point being made is parenthetical to the main argument.

This text went to press before the end of rehearsals and so may differ slightly from the play as performed.

ACT ONE

A church hall in an Oxfordshire village on December 24th. The usual things are there: a stage, curtains, wooden floor, possibly wooden walls, fold-away chairs and an air of being trapped in time since the 1940s.

A doorway to a small kitchen to one side.

The lights are dim. We might be able to see that the room has been decorated with a tree, tinsel, lights, baubles, the lot. ANDY*'s bought it all and put it up.*

There is also a home-made Christmas scene. A small house, with snow, and a pond outside.

ANDY *has pretty much finished all this decoration and now stands with his phone.*

ANDY   So when you arrive, I'll be here

well I won't be *here* I won't be just standing up waiting staring at the door that would be a bad first impression I'll be sat on a chair or through there in the kitchen with a coffee, but not on my phone that wouldn't look right too casual you should know that this is my focus, that this matters and I've made an effort which I have by the way.

By the time I'm finished, that should be obvious.

So no phone but I can't just be doing nothing so I'll… have my book, reading my book and then when you knock on the door you won't knock on the door I'll have the door open you can just walk in so okay, when you do I'll put the book down, stand up, you'll survey the scene and notice that I've been reading and that'll make it seem like I'm fresh and healthy and cultured and normal and not watching TV on my phone all the time like you probably imagine I am.

So you come in, book down, stand up, go over and greet you but at a distance.

The distance is important so it's clear I'm not expecting a kiss or hug 'don't worry' it needs to say 'I get it. Been a while', actually I'll say hi before I welcome you in so

Start again. You come in, book down, then *as* I stand up, 'Hi', a few steps towards, a deliberate stop and I say something maybe like 'come in'.

Casual. 'come in'

I thought this place rather than the house because it's neutral ground.

After I say 'come in' you'll probably walk a bit further into the room and I'll say like 'it's so good you've come' and then something to break the ice like 'god this is strange' no that's bad I'm not going to say that 'god this is strange' I'm such a moron I can see why you left if your dad's going to say banal things like that 'god this is strange'!

better off without me.

Maybe you'll *want* a hug or kiss so I need to be ready, cos if you are definitely going for those things then fine but the key is not to get carried away you left for a reason I expect no you *definitely* left for a reason you didn't just get *lost* one day so yes there's a reason and who knows if that reason has changed.

Whatever happens, I can't believe in a matter of minutes you'll walk through that door.

Maybe.

Probably.

He unpacks a Christmas jumper, with a pudding on the front.

Christmas jumper

take the edge off

Even you can't get angry if I'm wearing a pudding.

He puts it on.

Terry Scott wore a good one in the 1982 Terry and June Christmas special when his boss is accidentally invited round with his sex-obsessed secretary Miss Fennel and Terry's colleague Malcolm. It feels dated of course but it's a tight script and the point is all the way through Terry's in his Christmas jumper which mitigates any potential cruelty. It was on BBC Store for a while but they've shut BBC Store now so you'll have to order the DVD.

Except there's no way you own a DVD player. Actually you probably have no idea what half the words I just used are. You won't know who Terry Scott is. Well, you're missing out, that's all I can say.

'"DVD's"?! Jesus!' you'll think with a scornful tone of thought 'come on *Dad* we're *streaming* now?' and *I know* I can stream I *stream* but equally I like browsing selecting the DVD from its elaborate case kneeling down to insert it then sitting back and working through the various menus before getting to the thing you wanted to watch in the first place and yes I expect from your point of view this might be ancient and unappealing (much like myself) but for me it's exactly the joy. A slow and precise ritual, which I'm wilfully sticking with.

It's not all about being efficient, Maya.

I went to an HMV the other day, in Reading. The staff weren't as friendly as they used to be in the nineties. In the nineties I used to go there every Saturday, spent hours there like it was a club. Only bought something occasionally but it was the place you'd go. People talked to each other.

I'm not massively keen to say sorry. I mean I don't know what I'd be apologising for. I don't know what happened, you're the one who left, but I'm a little worried that's why you've come back.

You know what makes me think you're coming back? How I know? Maybe it's not obvious? Because from my side it's been quite a sequence of events and they've left me certain we're on the brink right on the *brink* of your reappearance. Like some *Neighbours* shock plot development – the actor playing you, their post-Ramsay Street career didn't work out so after one hit single and a couple of mediocre films they're back to Australia and they return to Erinsborough for a limited storyline but then it's so popular they stay for years it's like that.

About a week ago my friend Julie you remember Julie, with the neck, she's not a close friend but I've known her for ages since school kissed her once at a party in some village we got off in the utility room of this big house knocked the mops over I fancied her a lot then but now we're both old well not so much, which isn't rude because I'm sure that goes both ways anyway I bump into her outside WHSmiths and she says you must be happy I say no – yes – what? Do I look – no – what – Sorry?

She says because of Maya. What? Maya's back.

What? Maya's back. What?

Is she? What? Yeah don't you know? What?

She saw you in Turl Street Kitchen having coffee with someone last week and I'm I was I'm

I have two questions

Firstly what's Turl Street Kitchen? Apparently it's a café in central Oxford, I don't go into central Oxford much so fine that makes sense but secondly my second question and this is more important

Is she sure?

Because I've spent a long time trying not to hope.

Because to be disappointed every day when you don't come back is –

So if she's really saying she saw you back here back where you grew up then I need her to be absolutely one hundred per cent no-room-for-error certain.

She says without question

You looked different. But it was you.

She watched you talking to a friend she would have gone up to you but she didn't want to make you feel like you were being observed claustrophobic whatever, which I find well, really irritating actually, I wish she *had* gone up to you and found out more information any information but she didn't, she says she heard you speak but wasn't sure what about, she couldn't remember any of the words you used not a *single word* – as she's talking I'm remembering that Julie was always known for being good looking but on another planet one of those girls drifting around carried through life by the intoxicating fumes of being very physically attractive I've always wondered what happens to girls like that when they get older and they're not so attractive any more, sorry women not girls, actually if your misogyny alarm has gone off which it probably has then yes I'm sure this happens to good-looking men too, the same thing. This is not me talking about women. It's about what happens to physical attractiveness over time, okay?

Got to be so careful when talking to you…
I remember that.

Julie said sorry I assumed you knew she was back,
but at least this means she's alright?! Yeah? That
she's doing okay?

You looked a bit older apparently you were more
confident she said the way you were talking you
were gesturing passionately I wish I knew what
about.

I ask when was this, what time exactly? She says
a week ago Wednesday half-three, she was meeting
someone so she knows for sure what the time was.
Okay. I make to go, and Julia says oh and she had
a tattoo.

What? She had a tattoo on her back a tattoo a tattoo
okay what of what of what was it?

A bird.

What bird?

Julie's not an expert. It may not have been a bird.

It had wings that's all she can say.

I made my excuses and left.

Pause.

I'm pleased you sent that text the day you went.
At least I knew you hadn't been murdered.

I sent one back.

Actually I sent forty-seven back.

Not sure if you've seen it but our text conversation
looks a little one sided these days. If you weren't
aware of the context it would look like a stalker.

Surely you've changed your phone. Of course you
have.

But the number still rings. It's still a phone, still in use, so –

Anyway.

The Turl Street Kitchen.

Not café.

Not restaurant.

Kitchen. If you go there, you're eating in the kitchen.

It's a bit posh wooden floor wooden walls wooden facial expressions from the staff I don't know if this is a place you chose or the suggestion of your friend I can't imagine it's your kind of thing anyway I go in try to find where you order a coffee and walk through about three different rooms but eventually I find what could be a counter and speak to this young guy I'd say maybe probably he was a student who needs a job on the side he looks at me already thinking I'm not his usual clientele not wearing a good enough coat like already he can tell I'm going to be a hassle or maybe that's not true and he treats everyone with this level of contempt.

He doesn't go 'hi how can I help you?' 'what can I get you?' 'how are you?' none of that he glances up and goes 'hey'

'hey'

like I'm just a stranger in the street stood next to him not a potential customer in the place that pays his wages I'm sorry, you know this stuff always bothered me well it bothers me even more now, it's not about me having rights and being a customer it's about human decency and politeness the feeling those qualities are disappearing people don't know how to be kind to each other, they don't know the difference between right and wrong or worse, they *do* know the difference but they don't care – we should talk about that more, the things I watched when I was young, Spielberg, *Knight Rider*, they have a clear sense of who's right and who's wrong and I know it's fashionable to say everything is somewhere in the middle but actually I think that's just letting everyone off the hook, up to the point where like that YouTuber – he's – can't remember his name, about your age, anyway he posts a video where he finds – Logan Paul! he posts a video of a BODY he's found in the woods someone that's committed suicide and he doesn't DO anything about it or act appropriately he just kind of makes jokes and laughs then puts it up for the world to see, you heard about that right – and it's not even when other people react with horror that he does anything about it it's when he starts to lose viewers or whatever and YouTube says he might lose his income *that's* the moment he says he regrets it although he clearly doesn't and I think if you want to know, that's the thing I worry the most about you and your generation that you're so focused on getting the language right about identity that you don't have a clear sense of *morality* don't you think if YouTube existed in the thirties in Germany that's exactly the sort of video you'd get from the Nazi teenagers take a lesson from history Maya, take a lesson from me, the creeping collapse of interior morality the normalisation of violence and sadism the collapse of basic human dignity that's what I see with so many of your generation the good ones focusing on the wrong things and the bad ones the growing number of bad ones gaining in power and succeeding in normalising what even five years ago was horrific.

'hey'

This Nazi in the Turl Street Kitchen.

I say I'm looking for my daughter she was here last Wednesday at 3.30 p.m. I wondered if anyone might have seen her I describe you but as I'm talking this guy is just staring at me, he's already checked out of our conversation when I didn't just ask for a coffee. He's not paid to listen to this – he's physically taken a step away and *this* is what I mean about right and wrong it's the right thing to help someone who seems in distress but all he's thinking about is his *function*, his *day*, I see him take this step away from me and I just stop. Stop halfway through a –

He says I don't work Wednesdays. With a Third Reich sneer, this white posh floppy blond Mini Boris, standing there in his T-shirt and apron, looking like he might break into 'Tomorrow Belongs to Me'.

Thank God someone else comes over, and she's very different, actually with her smile and energy and the way her hair falls she reminds me of your mum.

Which isn't massively helpful right in this moment. But she's kind, she's the assistant manager and she says yes she was working last Wednesday I tell her the situation, describe you best as I can and Not-Mum says did you have any distinguishing features I said you apparently had a tattoo on your upper back.

Of what?

It had wings.

A bird?

We don't know.

What?

Well it's not just birds that have wings.

What else then?

Bats.

You think she had a tattoo of a bat?

I don't know what it was.

Unicorns have wings too. Some of them.

I can't argue with that. Let's add unicorns to the list.

We work out where you must've been sat and she tries but eventually says she just doesn't remember she serves a hundred people a day.

As she says sorry she smiles sympathetically, lowers her face. If she fancied me this would be the moment I would have got a flicker but there's nothing of course of *course* I mean it's ridiculous to even be having those thoughts but I am I mean I'm a man it's inevitable, aren't men supposed to think about sex every five seconds or something? Probably not allowed to talk about how often you think about sex these days. Put you in jail.

Anyway though, in my case it is totally ridiculous. Especially in the face of someone properly attractive and nice like her I mean I do own a mirror I am aware of the inadequacy of the offering the massive aesthetic hurdle someone would have to clear before they could even start to contemplate being intimate with me.

I say sorry but do you have CCTV? She says yes but she can't give it to me she's not being funny but the problem is she doesn't know who I am. What if I could prove who I was, then maybe – 'Look,' she says and she seems a bit awkward 'the problem is we don't know if she *wants* you to contact her in fact well it sounds like she *could* contact you but she hasn't so...'

He shrugs, like she did.

He shrugs again, like a mockery of it.

But no, that's a fair point a very fair point.

I turn around and I'm walking out but then this woman comes back after me puts a hand on my arm which if I'm honest makes me think of Columbo 'just one more thing' and brilliantly she nearly says that, she says 'One thing more you could try.' She says try Esther.

Esther?

Esther comes in mid-afternoon every other day she might've been here on Wednesday, she's there over there in the corner and I look and there's a woman mid-seventies sat on her own I say mid-seventies, I have no idea, she could be fifty she could be a hundred I find age very hard with people over forty-five or younger than thirty I can't tell at all and just to say the other distracting thing is that she looks like Esther Rantzen. She looks a lot a *lot* like Esther Rantzen, she's called Esther and that's who she looks like, I mean just to be clear she's *not* Esther Rantzen she looks different enough to be sure of that but it's close enough to be really weird like she's an Esther Rantzen tribute-act person or something anyway I try to put that out of my head as it's not relevant.

The assistant manager introduces me to Esther-not-Rantzen and I tell her the whole thing and she listens and eventually says yes actually she does remember them because they were having this intense conversation the other girl, she was crying at one point.

I write down my number and ask her to call me immediately if she sees either of the girls again. She looks at me, says she will, then suddenly asks 'Why did your daughter leave?'

I say I don't know Esther, I don't know why she left but

Well…

That's life.

Not a flicker.

She says she'll text me if she sees either of them again.

I couldn't do any more couldn't think of what else I could do and anyway I had a date with Polly.

A date yes stop laughing trying to move on, you don't know Polly met her through a mutual friend this is actually the second date and the problem is I didn't enjoy the previous one and the bigger problem is I don't enjoy dates at all, it's not a world I grew up in partly because we, people my age, we never really did dating, I remember many conversations in my twenties about how 'dating' was an American thing and the Brits just got drunk and got off instead which admittedly I can see in the cold light of 2018 feels a bit problematic when it comes to consent, so yes I understand dating is on paper better but in reality when you're my age and you've never done it, never been trained in it – look stop laughing. Try to understand cos I'm being open here and if you've never done it it's really stressful and it's not helped by the fact that the women are my age which means most of them are also just as useless at it for all the same reasons. Watching two people of my age trying to figure out a 'date' is like watching two pensioners trying to use Snapchat.

So the first went badly but god knows if that's Polly's fault really. She sort of teased me, which is fine and she's genuinely funny, and she clearly likes me, well, she wanted to meet again and normally you know I love a bit of, banter, whatever, but I came away from the last one – she went on about my shirt, I was wearing this white

shirt like completely white and she said she had to
make sure she didn't confuse me with the waiter
I tried to play along but I was self-conscious for the
rest of the evening. Didn't enjoy it much.

But I said I would do it again, and I thought better
not cancel. George from work said to keep on
casting the net that you never know so I put on as
normal a shirt as I have and head out we're meeting
at this curry place in Summertown informal her
suggestion and it's okay and I think she knew the
shirt thing hurt so she says I look nice and doesn't
do so much teasing, the whole evening is fine it's
fine but it's like mocking is her language like the
only way she knows how to be funny, and now
she's sensed I don't like it now that's been taken
away from her she hasn't got anything except
trying to be sincere and she hasn't got much to say
so she just seems a bit alone like me and a bit –
well we both seem desperate and I like her more
now the mocking's gone I think actually she's a
good person we could be friends but there is
literally no way on earth, and she clearly feels this
too, that we're ever going to get with each other.

Is that what you would say? We would've said
Shag, Bonk, but I believe you say 'Get with each
other'? Is that right?

The way you talk about it is much cooler. By which
I don't mean more fashionable, I mean it's of a
lower temperature.

Anyway, her ex-husband Richard slept with a
woman he met on a stag do, kept on meeting her and
lied about it for three years, then she found out.
They've got an eleven-year-old son called Jack
I found myself thinking a lot as she was saying how
bad it was well small mercies at least Richard didn't
die and at least you've still got Jack. I didn't tell her
anything about Mum and all of that and I didn't tell

her anything about you because I've learnt it's too much. You tell people and they think you're going to infect them with that burden somehow, it doesn't lend itself to a sexy atmosphere so I didn't mention any of it but it did mean I resented hearing about her perfectly normal separation and then I hated myself for resenting it and thought what a terrible person I am you can see why this date went badly.

She made a small house on the table with poppadoms that was impressive and funny I found it sort of reckless until the waiter came over didn't smile or show any emotional reaction at all he just swiped the whole thing off the table onto his tray picked up an empty glass and left it felt so violent and without humour we both tried to smile at each other but probably that was the moment we knew the night wasn't working when any last remaining embers of possibility had been conclusively extinguished.

On the way home I pass Thomas Cook and they've changed the image of the couple in the window, they do that every month now, it's two people in their early thirties embracing in warm tropical water they look like they're not aware of anything except each other not responsibility rent tax work borders wars age sudden diagnosis of cancer that takes you completely by surprise and kills your wife in five months and leaves your family totally in pieces without any reference point all your dreams gone all you hoped for – yeah this Thomas Cook couple they aren't aware of any of that.

Maya just admit it, yeah? That whatever the reason you left it must've had something to do with Mum because everything after Mum is to do with her and maybe I didn't do the right thing behave in the right way but surely you can forgive me that? Even if you can't at least you could give me the chance to talk about it.

But maybe you're not coming back. Maybe you were in Oxford for some completely different reason, and you're not getting my messages and I'm going to end up here, in a church hall, alone, surrounded by three hundred pounds' worth of Christmas decorations and a model of a home that doesn't exist any more.

Anyway so… then, what's led up to all this specifically is, I'm at work yesterday with George and Suze and along with all the normal museum work there's an idea we might refresh the Anglo-Saxon exhibit. And I can see why, you might remember it, you probably don't but it was made in nineteen-seventy-something and basically it's a shop dummy wearing what looks like a kilt made out of a sack his arm is in the air for reasons no one understands, including him as his face doesn't seem aware of what his arm is doing and around him it's like he's dropped a load of completely random objects and hasn't noticed – the objects are the Anglo-Saxon finds but it just looks like he's just had a kind of midlife crisis, thrown all his possessions everywhere and put his arm up so compared with some of the more recent additions he's probably had his time and we need a new Anglo-Saxon centrepiece. Suze says we should outsource get a company in to do it professionally George feels part of the charm of the museum is that it's local and we should engage the community in helping create something unique. I'm acting as peacekeeper. I suspect the community answer will make something more worthy and more shit but the quotes to get an outside company in are ridiculous so… anyway this is all going on, Suze is getting heated when I get a text from a number I don't recognise it just says '*she's here again.*'

I tell them I'm feeling unwell and I've got to leave. Now.

I've never done this before, not even during
everything with Mum. George starts to go, 'mate
can I just ask one more – ' but Suze can see the
look on my face and just says yeah you go.

So I run out and can't see a bus so I go to the taxi
company three doors down and say I need a taxi
now and they say it'll be ten minutes and I say no
I need one now it's the *middle of the day* what are
your taxis all doing where are they and they tell me
not to get aggressive that if I've got their app that
might be the quickest thing but I... I'm *there*, I'm
physically *there* in the office so how would using
an *app* make any sense so I come back out and put
my hand up to try to hail a cab but as I do my
phone and wallet which I hadn't put in my pocket
properly they fall on the floor and I realise I'm
standing there like this Anglo-Saxon man

my hand in the air surrounded by his possessions
having a crisis.

A man who's had his time.

I'm picking up my stuff when a taxi pulls in by the
firm I run up to him and he agrees and I think now
we're talking, but we're going into town at just
thirty miles an hour. I think about telling him why
I need to get there, maybe he could make an
exception and put his foot down like Tim
McInnerny in *Notting Hill* – 'Right!' zigzag
through the traffic but I don't ask, I couldn't bear
the likely reality of him just nodding, then
complaining about traffic so I'm silent instead,
waiting, thinking what if I get there and you've
gone again and that's it.

The taxi gets to where it has to turn right off the
High and I say I'll jump out I pay him run across
the Camera, the cobbles, faster than I've ever run,
this middle-aged man, coach parties of tourists and

shoppers staring at me laughing 'what could ever make him run like that?'

You used to see people run all the time, maybe before mobile phones people were more likely to miss things, whereas now you'd just text.

You hardly ever see adults run these days.

Except when there's terrorists. That's the only time I've seen it on the news then you see people really run so maybe me running like that was irresponsible I could have caused a stampede ending up with hundreds of people running through Oxford unsure what they're escaping but not willing to take the risk to look behind them just running just running behind this man who looks like the world's going to end.

I get to Turl Street Kitchen, out of breath, I look to see you but I can't, I check all the rooms and eventually find Esther sat in her seat.

She says you've gone again.

I...

I got here as fast as I could.

Yes says Esther I can see that, you're sweating from everywhere. I realise she's right 'You look disgusting' she says and I just stare at her, offended, but then I catch myself in the mirror and realise she's completely right my grey hair is matted to my blotchy, overweight face my shirt has sweat patches everywhere my trousers don't stay up because of my belly and my coat is just shit it's a shit coat I hate it Esther Rantzen is completely fucking right I'm old and I'm on my own and I'm disgusting.

'Sorry not disgusting,' she says 'desperate you look *desperate*.' She apologises, she gets her words mixed up a bit these days 'you're desperate aren't you that's why you ran so fast.'

Yes I tell her yes I am

'Well then' says Esther with a cheeky smile 'it's lucky I spoke to her'

'You did?'

'I explained who I was, what I know, and she looked like she wanted to leave so I quickly asked her "are you going to see your dad? Because he's desperate to see you".'

'And,' Esther says, 'your daughter didn't say anything in reply, she just left.'

Esther smiles. Great big perfect teeth, but I'm not sure why she's smiling.

'Don't you see?' She says. 'When I asked her that question, she didn't reply. She could have said no. But she *didn't reply.*'

And I realise she's right. It would have been the easiest thing for you to say no. 'No way am I seeing my dad, I hate him,' but you didn't. You just left and that made me think that you *are* here to see me. But you're waiting, maybe. For the big day. So close to Christmas, it can't be a coincidence…

You're not sure how to go about it maybe. Maybe you're plucking up the courage, or need some gesture from me, I don't know but that's when I thought of doing this.

A big Christmas olive branch.

So if you do want to see me, you get the right message. That I love you, and desperately want you back in my life. And at the very least you know you were seen and the message got back to me. You know I'm keen to see you. I know you know that.

So I take the time off work, call about the hall – no one's using it on Christmas Eve. It only cost ten quid. They were surprised to hear from me. It's been a while since I've spoken to any of them. It was Gilly. You remember her? I didn't say what I was using it for, just a gathering and she didn't ask any other questions.

But she asked after you. Said she missed Mum. That they all still think of her.

Didn't you think it was cruel? To leave me on my own. I've coped pretty well, but eventually, maybe not tonight, but eventually have a think because, the thing is – maybe I'm due an apology as well.

Anyway. I got the decorations. Then, as you hopefully know, I left another message on the phone you haven't answered in two years, and told you the plan. Texted you. Left a note on the front door. That if you want to see me, you could come here, neutral ground, no strings, no expectations. Just a place we can meet. Familiar, but not too familiar.

And yeah.

For better or worse, whether you know it or not.

Here I am.

Ready for Christmas.

Because Christmas.

With baubles and trees and little snowy houses.

Well…

That's when they say people come home.

He looks at the scene for a moment. Then picks up the switch and presses it, expecting it to come to life.

Nothing happens.

He looks at the four-way it is connected to, then goes off, into the kitchen where it's plugged in.

A moment.

There's movement behind the exterior door. Through the window, we can see a figure. It looks like a young woman.

The door opens and she comes in.

A young woman, mid-twenties.

She's carrying a big box. Switches on the lights, and we can see the hall more clearly now. Particularly a large banner which says 'Welcome Home'.

The woman looks round, surprised.

As she comes into the room, the door shuts behind her.

Having heard this, ANDY runs in.

He stops when he sees her.

Oh.

NATALIE   Hi.

ANDY   Oh.

NATALIE   Were you –

ANDY   Sorry –

NATALIE   I'm Natalie.

ANDY   Natalie?

NATALIE   Natalie yeah.

           Were you expecting someone else?

           Blackout.

           End of Act One.

ACT TWO

We pick up from exactly where we left off –

NATALIE   You were thinking someone else would walk in.

ANDY   What? I don't

NATALIE   You did a face

ANDY   A / face?

NATALIE   You looked like (*expression*) yeah like (*expression*) like you were expecting a different person like I'm a disappointment

ANDY   What? Sorry how can I / help you?

NATALIE   I'm picking up the stuff.

ANDY   What stuff?

NATALIE   The stuff from the kitchen didn't anyone tell you?

Clearly not. Got an email, Mum forwarded it when she told me what to do. Look.

She holds up her phone.

'Not a problem at all, you can collect it on Christmas Eve, we need it back by the 28th as there's a party for the Rotundary Club.'

ANDY   Rotary Club.

NATALIE   Yeah. Cutlery, plates…

ANDY   You need it tonight?

NATALIE   We need it tomorrow actually (Christmas Day?) but I'm picking it up now. They said no one was using it.

ANDY   It was a late booking.

NATALIE   This is / pretty!

ANDY   I called Gilly yesterday / and she said –

NATALIE   Who's coming home? Gilly didn't mention we
           were nicking all the stuff?

ANDY   She didn't say anything about anything.

NATALIE   She's getting too old for admin, don't you think?

ANDY   You… you know her?

NATALIE   Yeah from back in the day, before I went to uni.
           She swears so much? When she thinks no one's
           listening. Once I came out of the toilet, caught her
           calling the coffee machine a cunt. Bit rude.

ANDY   I… I can't imagine Gilly using that kind of
           language.

NATALIE   Someone's been away then? Holiday? Prison?

ANDY   No.

NATALIE   When's everyone getting here? Bit late to start.
           Eight-fifteen already.

ANDY   It's… not a party. I'm only surprising one person.
           It's just me and this other person.

NATALIE   That's sweet.

ANDY   And I'd rather when they get here we were alone
           so –

NATALIE   Man? Woman?

ANDY   So if that's okay?

NATALIE   You…

           Oh right you want me to go?

ANDY   Just because this is a private thing, you understand?

NATALIE   Oh. Yeah okay. I do. I get it.

           Beat.

It's just Mum's got twenty people coming for lunch I don't know where she gets them from, half are family, a quarter are old people who'd be on their own and the other quarter, well, not a clue, she's mad but I said I would and now I'm here I might as well just pick it all up, if that's okay?

ANDY   Will it take long?

NATALIE   To collect it? Nah, I'll go in there, make a cup of tea, pack it up –

ANDY   Wait –

NATALIE   – get it out to the car. Twenty, twenty-five minutes can't see it / lasting longer than that.

ANDY   A cup of tea?

NATALIE   Half an hour? Yeah cup of tea it's really cold out there you been out there? Come on you don't have to do anything and when your mum gets here I'm sure she'll understand.

ANDY   It's not my mum.

NATALIE   Not your mum okay, ruling that one out –

ANDY   Look, I –

NATALIE   I might also have a wee at some point but once that's done and I have the stuff, this is all yours, to welcome that special person back into your life – man, woman or other, I'll be gone and you'll have the whole evening to do whatever you two want to do together.

ANDY   It's not a relationship, it's not –

NATALIE   Seriously dude I don't mind what you're doing it's your private business I respect the fact that it's a secret –

ANDY   It's not a secret.

NATALIE   Well you're not telling me so –

ANDY   I don't know you.

NATALIE   Let's not argue you're not telling me ergo secret on
            some level but that's fine whatever you get up to is
            okay with me so recap: In. Tea. Pack stuff. Possible
            wee. Gone. Deal?

            A moment.

ANDY   Just please be as quick as you can.

NATALIE   Totally.

            So you bought all this stuff, put it up?

ANDY   Yes.

NATALIE   love it, like a garden centre, what's this?

ANDY   It's a model.

NATALIE   Yeah I can see that. What of?

ANDY   …

NATALIE   Love your jumper too. Pudding. Wait – does it have
            lights?

ANDY   Yes but it's –

            *She presses the button on the remote. Nothing
            happens.*

NATALIE   Oh.

ANDY   The… plugs aren't working. Don't know why. Must
            be the circuit. Haven't found the right switch…

NATALIE   So it's not a date what is it then?

ANDY   The kitchen's through there.

NATALIE   A mate or something?

ANDY   A… family member actually but –

NATALIE   'Family member' no problem. Right. Kitchen.

            She goes into the kitchen.

ANDY   Sorry I would help but I want to be ready when she
            comes.

NATALIE   'She.' Interesting.

            ANDY*'s annoyed at the slip-up. A moment. He
            checks his watch.*

            Light doesn't work in here, maybe it's on the same
            circuit as your sockets, you mind if I bring it all out
            there to pack?

ANDY   I... just... as quickly as you can. Please.

            She comes out with a pile of plates. On top is an
            X-Files *book.*

NATALIE   Is this yours? It was on the side.

ANDY   Yes.

NATALIE   Thought *X-Files* was a TV show?

ANDY   They made books as well.

NATALIE   And James Bond.

ANDY   What?

NATALIE   James Bond bookmark.

ANDY   Sorry can you –

NATALIE   Two women's legs and a little James Bond standing
            between them, underneath. I presume it's supposed
            to be sexy but it's more like this woman's just shat
            out a tiny Sean Connery. The seventies were so
            weird.

ANDY   It's Roger Moore actually.

NATALIE   You like it though? 'Bond.'

ANDY   Yes.

NATALIE   Why?

ANDY   It's fun.

NATALIE   Fun in a sort of very sexist way?

ANDY   Well, yes Bond has always been presented as
          sexist. Old-fashioned. That's part of the character.
          Even in the –

          She goes out again.

NATALIE   Racist too you seen that one with the voodoo dude?

ANDY   Baron Samedi.

NATALIE   Wow yeah you know his name big fan clearly you
          seen that one then?

ANDY   It's of its time.

NATALIE   Well that is true 'of its time'.

ANDY   Right.

          She comes back in with another pile of plates.

NATALIE   And its time was really very racist indeed. Sister.
          It's your sister!

ANDY   No. Is that everything? Because you said –

NATALIE   Yeah that's all of it.

ANDY   Good.

NATALIE   Is she coming right now, this woman, literally this
          second?

ANDY   I don't know. Not being funny but I've got a plan
          tonight and you're not –

          She goes out again to the kitchen.

          I thought you said that was everything?

NATALIE   You've forgotten haven't you?

ANDY   I'm sorry?

NATALIE   Milk?

ANDY   I... Oh, no. Please.

NATALIE   I'm making one either way – what's your name?

ANDY   …Andy.

NATALIE   Andy we agreed on the tea that was what we said
           so I'm making it either way so if you want one it
           won't make this any longer I promise so if you do
           want one how do you want it?

           Pause.

ANDY   Milk.

NATALIE   Sugar?

ANDY   Two.

NATALIE   Two! Old-school. Brave. You laugh in the face of
           diabetes.

           A moment. ANDY *aware it might be useful for him
           to help pack the stuff up, but equally not wanting to
           get involved.*

ANDY   You want me to help with this stuff?

NATALIE   No. You're alright.

           NATALIE *comes back out with two cups of tea.
           Gives one to* ANDY.

ANDY   Thanks.

NATALIE   No problem.

           She sips her tea then sets to work.

           So how racist are you then?

ANDY   What?

NATALIE   It's normally manageable if you know up front, it's
           when you've got to like someone and then it turns
           out they're a massive Nazi –

ANDY   I'm not racist.

NATALIE   Yeah but all white people if they've been brought
           up in this country they are a bit, even if it's just
           ignorance, and you love that voodoo Bond film –

ANDY   I don't. And I'm not.

NATALIE   Okay.

            She drinks her tea.

            What about sexism then? Your level of misogyny.

ANDY   What sort of person comes out and asks a man
            they've just met if they're a racist and misogynist?

NATALIE   Someone surrounded by racists and misogynists.

ANDY   Which you think you are?

NATALIE   Yeah.

ANDY   Why? Where were you at university?

NATALIE   Britain.

            Beat. He smiles at her.

ANDY   Well, no, you can relax, I'm not racist, misogynist,
            transphobic, Islamophobic whatever I'm just
            a normal guy on Christmas Eve doing my own
            thing –

            She holds up the X-Files *book. Smiles.*

NATALIE   No offence mate but I wouldn't call this normal –

            He takes it off her and puts it down on the table.

ANDY   Thank you, for the tea, but you really do need to go
            a bit faster, please, if you can.

NATALIE   Because of your daughter.

ANDY   What?

NATALIE   It's your daughter who's coming home. Right?
            It's high stakes as you're nervous, we know it's
            a woman but not your mum or sister so the next
            logical guess. Right?

            *A moment. He looks at her and doesn't deny it. She
            stops packing.*

You don't see her much, split up with her mum and she's coming over for Christmas so you want to get it right. That's why you're anxious.

ANDY   Yes.

NATALIE   Yeah. There you go. That's sweet. Don't worry, if she comes I'll clear out.

Yeah. I'm getting it now.

There's a… rift between you, right?

ANDY

NATALIE   What happened?

Why did she go?

What did you do?

ANDY looks at her.

You don't have to tell me.

But you can if you want.

Cos I'm here.

And I'm good at listening. Really good. Look.

She looks at him. 'Listening.' He stares at her.

He looks at her, looks at the clock, then goes to the front door, opens it and looks out. Pause.

ANDY   I don't know.

He shuts the door and comes back over.

I don't have any idea why she went.

NATALIE   Right.

Beat.

ANDY   I'll give you a hand.

NATALIE   Great.

He starts to help her wrap everything in paper, and package it up.

So…

So how did you vote?

ANDY   What?

NATALIE   Making conversation. What was it? In, out?

ANDY   Oh I… Look, no, I'm sorry I'm not… not getting in to –

NATALIE   Leave. I knew it.

ANDY   No, I didn't say –

NATALIE   Didn't need to.

She holds up the X-Files *book.*

This was a clue.

ANDY   How?

NATALIE   Two white people scared of aliens.

He takes it off her again.

ANDY   I don't particularly want to / get in to it.

NATALIE   There's three possible answers when you ask someone the question, either they go Remain straight away or they go it's a private decision in which case it's obviously Leave or there's a small group who immediately just come out and say 'Leave actually' but most of that lot are actually racists and you said you're not a racist so that puts you in the middle group. 'Leave'.

           How are you feeling about it all now?

ANDY   Good, actually.

NATALIE   I'm really depressed.

ANDY   Well you shouldn't be so scared.

NATALIE   Depressed I said, not scared.

            You haven't seen her for a long time have you?

ANDY   I…

            No. Two years.

NATALIE   She went after you split up with her mum?

ANDY   Her mum died.

NATALIE   Oh. Whoa. Sorry.

ANDY   Yeah. Five years ago.

NATALIE   Then after that your daughter lived with you but
            then one day she just left.

            Where did she go?

            And what makes you think she's coming back
            now? Has she called?

            ANDY *keeps on wrapping and packing. He
            actually quite likes the activity. The distraction.*

ANDY   Someone saw her in town a few days ago, and
            when asked if she was planning to contact me…
            she didn't say no. Which I know sounds like not
            much to go on but –

            When her mum died I couldn't imagine being a
            family again. It seems stupid now but I couldn't
            picture any more family celebrations so I threw all
            the Christmas decorations away. Every year we'd
            make a little Christmas scene. I threw them away too.

            So yesterday I thought –

            I thought if she wants to – make contact again –
            this might be a –

            Doesn't matter. Nothing to you with you. Not
            interested.

NATALIE   Might be a what?

ANDY   This is honestly none of your business.

NATALIE   What's her name?

           Beat.

ANDY   Maya.

NATALIE   That's a nice name.

           Come on, you must have had some thoughts about
           why she went?

           ANDY *doesn't reply. He drinks his tea. Then
           carries on packing.*

ANDY   Maybe I said something. I don't know. There wasn't
           anything obvious, or big, that happened. I was just
           having a normal day then I get this message from
           her saying she's gone.

NATALIE   And nothing since?

ANDY   No.

NATALIE   But you reckon tonight's the night.

ANDY

NATALIE   Even though she hasn't actually made any kind of
           contact?

ANDY

NATALIE   Don't you think if she planned to see you she'd call
           you first or something, an email, or whatever just to
           check you were going to be here check you wanted
           to see her and –

ANDY   Look I don't want to / talk about it with you
           really –

NATALIE   Don't you think if she was going to come back she
           would rather it was on her own terms? That *she*
           decided where, when and how – not being told what
           to do and the whole being sort of… staged, by you.

ANDY   You're saying you think this was all a mistake?

NATALIE   Depends, what sort of person is she? Does she like surprises?

ANDY   I don't know. I clearly didn't know who she was then, let alone now. I'm guessing. This is all a guess.

NATALIE   But you love her.

ANDY   I...

            He smiles.

NATALIE   What? What's funny?

ANDY   Only a girl of your age would ask that question.

NATALIE   What question.

ANDY   If a father loves his daughter.

NATALIE   Why?

ANDY   Because all fathers love their daughters.

NATALIE   All...? Huh. No.

ANDY   The vast majority –

NATALIE   Actually a vast lot don't. My question is completely valid you know how many really shit fathers there are out there?

ANDY   Well I'm not a shit father.

            I'm really not.

            ANDY *looks towards the door. The time. The lack of power for the lights, the mess of packing on the table. He's upset.*

            Look – sorry – honestly this is beyond you this whole thing that's going on with me, no offence but it's so completely beyond your life experience.

NATALIE   How do you know?

ANDY   Because you seem... can I be honest with you, sorry I don't know your name.

NATALIE   I told you.

ANDY   I didn't hear.

NATALIE   Natalie Woods.

ANDY   Okay 'Natalie' you seem naive – asking the
questions you're asking, the way you speak, it's
sort of wonderful but it reads as very young.

NATALIE   Maybe to you. Most people just find me open,
honest, funny –

ANDY   Well yes you certainly seem honest but –

NATALIE   Naive? Not more than most people. What I haven't
experienced I try to encounter, best I can. Cos
most lives aren't like this, most evenings not as
benign, and even in our massively cushioned lives
we'll be lucky if we don't experience real horror at
some point.

ANDY   Happy Christmas Natalie.

NATALIE   Yeah well it's worth knowing how lucky we are.

ANDY   I don't feel lucky.

NATALIE   Yeah but you should. Is what I'm saying.

    Beat.

    You really don't know why she left?

    You really haven't even got a guess? Come on,
you've had years.

    Beat.

ANDY   You asked about the vote.

NATALIE   Yeah.

ANDY   Yeah. So that's…

    That's the closest I've got: because the vote was
two weeks before she went. She was very pro-
Europe, very in to Europe, I think she assumed
I was going to vote her way then I told her I hadn't

and – it was a few days after – she'd been to
Glastonbury and got worked up about it with
everyone there I think then she came back here to
her gap-year job and was really sad and I said
maybe it won't be so bad you know and she said
what? I said you know I voted to Leave?

And she – I knew she'd be surprised but she looked
totally betrayed I mean it was – well – we're
talking about essentially an economic almost
administrative thing here, I'm not saying it's not
important but it's not going to be the end of the
world so –

NATALIE   It is the end of the world.

ANDY   Yeah well it's not a surprise you would think that
but –

NATALIE   – a whole landscape of possibility / has
disappeared –

ANDY   – either way if she left because of that I just really
wouldn't know what to say because what was she
running away from? I mean I'm not exactly the
only one who voted that way, we were in the
majority and she has to respect that.

NATALIE   She doesn't. I don't. I believe in *parliamentary*
democracy not direct democratic rule anyone who
knows anything about government knows that's a
disaster and this is a classic example, it's a very
technical very complicated question –

ANDY   Yeah okay – look –

NATALIE   – to which the correct answer requires huge
knowledge of politics, economics, society, law,
security, none of which hardly anyone has so on
both sides we're totally unqualified, but at least
those of us for staying had the evidence that it was
basically working.

ANDY   Really? You think it was working?

NATALIE   No third world war, comparative economic
          prosperity, a strengthening of human rights, of course
          there are problems but we've been doing alright.

ANDY   'Doing alright' about sums it up. This country has
          huge reserves and talents and skills and we're
          already a union, we don't need to be tethered to
          another, less democratic more malfunctioning one.
          We were on our own for the previous fifteen
          hundred years before 1973 and we flourished. I think
          to be so certain it's the right thing to stay in shows
          a lack of perspective and, I'm sorry to say, another
          sign of naivety, but this is not the point –

NATALIE   What do you do for a living?

ANDY   I work in a museum.

NATALIE   A museum?

ANDY   Yes.

NATALIE   Makes sense.

ANDY   What does that mean?

NATALIE   I mean that from the evidence on display here,
          from your clothes, the subjects of conversation,
          your vision of the country, and also apparently your
          occupation I think you spend most of your time
          thinking about the past.

          But that's not where we are. Is it?

          *A moment. They look at each other. He sees her
          tattoo.*

ANDY   What's that of? Your… tattoo.

NATALIE   A horse. I always wanted to ride horses but I can't
          because of my back.

ANDY   Maya has a tattoo apparently.

NATALIE   Really?

ANDY   My friend who saw her told me. She said it had
            wings. So it's probably a bird.

            But obviously it could be a bat. Or a unicorn.

NATALIE   Or an angel.

ANDY   ...Right. Yes. I suppose so.

NATALIE   If she were to come back and see you, I expect
            she's worried that things haven't changed.

ANDY   What do you mean?

NATALIE   Let's imagine she's considering coming tonight.
            I would guess she's worried that whatever the
            reason is – that she left – has remained the same.
            That whatever you did to her then, you'll do it now.

ANDY   'Did to her'? I haven't done anything to her. Look,
            thanks for trying to help but maybe can you go
            now. Do the rest tomorrow.

NATALIE   I could take a guess? Why she left. I mean I've only
            just met you but the kindness of strangers yeah?

ANDY   You're what – twenty-five years old?

NATALIE   Twenty-four.

            Beat.

ANDY   Twenty-four years old, twenty minutes in the room
            with me, and you have a theory.

NATALIE   Yeah I do.

ANDY   Alright but before you offer it there are two
            thoughts in my head Natalie. Firstly there's the
            hope that your generation is actually better, just
            better. I mean you drink less, you do less crime,
            take less drugs than we did, you're all doing better
            at schooling and all of that, and now you're
            creating these social campaigns which genuinely
            seem to be changing things. The hope that you're
            bright young, wonderful things and I should just sit

back, enjoy it, listen to your theory, learn from you
and try to be better myself.

NATALIE   Sounds good.

ANDY   Yeah. But the other thought is that you're the
cabaret performers of the Weimar Republic,
playing with sexual identity with the Nazis just
round the corner, you're the activists on Twitter
during the Arab Spring, full of hope as they
overthrow dictators but totally unable to find a
regime strong enough to fill the gap so leaving their
countries open to army generals and gangsters.
You're a generation who's winning at what they
know they can win at, sexual freedoms, gender
identity, anti-misogyny, anti-racism, all relatively
easy things to argue for. But you're less good at
talking about class, economics, capitalism, fascism
the rise of popularism. I wonder if my generation
was more focused on those things because when
we talked to our grandparents they told us what it
was like to be bombed from the skies by fascists.
When you talked to your grandparents they
regurgitated the homophobia they'd read on the
front page of the *Daily Mail*.

NATALIE   Not my grandparents.

Beat.

ANDY   I know your intentions are good but... I wonder...

I don't want to be patronising, but...

Beat.

NATALIE   Finished?

Beat.

ANDY   Yes.

Go on then. What's your guess?

NATALIE   Tell me about when you said how you'd voted –

ANDY   What?

NATALIE   Tell me exactly what happened.

ANDY   I told her and she looked betrayed. Like, hurt.

NATALIE   Then what?

ANDY   Then I told her why. That we'd given the EU
            enough time to get their house in order and there
            comes a point where instead of being bullied, you
            have to stand up for what you believe in –

NATALIE   She listened.

ANDY   She screwed up her face a few times to make it
            clear she didn't agree with what I was saying but –

NATALIE   Did she interrupt?

ANDY   No.

NATALIE   And then?

ANDY   Then she started to make her arguments about why
            the European Union was a good thing.

NATALIE   Did you listen?

ANDY   Yes.

NATALIE   You didn't interrupt?

ANDY   Interrupt no but there were some things I disputed –

NATALIE   So you did interrupt.

ANDY   I pointed them out.

NATALIE   – but she kept going.

ANDY   Yes, she *definitely* kept going she started to get off
            the economy and tangible benefits like that and she
            started instead to talk, I don't know, culturally, like
            what it said about us as a nation and that we should
            have a desire – actually I remember this almost
            exactly – that we 'should have a desire eventually
            not to have borders at all and live in a completely
            different way.' I mean...

NATALIE   Why did you use a sarcastic voice just then?

ANDY   I… didn't.

NATALIE   Yes you used a –

ANDY   I'm relating it, quoting her. She was saying we shouldn't have borders at all, that she wanted to stay in just for a sort of cultural *feeling* of being the same.

NATALIE   So what did you say?

ANDY   I said that was all lovely, but that she needed to think about the real world.

NATALIE   Were you patronising?

ANDY   No.

NATALIE   Cos that sounded pretty patronising.

ANDY   Only if you're not confident in what you believe.

          Beat.

NATALIE   Did you laugh?

ANDY   Did I laugh?

NATALIE   Just then you smiled when you told me what she said. Did you laugh at it, at the time, with her?

ANDY   I… Yes I probably did, I mean it's quite a laughable thing that we should be working to not have any borders at all.

NATALIE   Why is that laughable?

ANDY   Well if you don't know –

NATALIE   No I don't know –

ANDY   Then you should read the entire history of the last two hundred years Natalie, you should protect your idealism cos it's great but consider that other people have been alive longer than you and balance it against the probability of your ignorance in certain subjects. You have the air of being a bit smug.

And it's not appealing. At all. To seem like you
know everything. Because you don't you can't, and
that certainty you perform that's the greatest sign
of ignorance.

You're clever yes but you're not wise.

Because there's a… depth of emotion here. In me.
That you're not responding to at all, that I'm not
sure you've noticed. You want to get into a
discussion about Brexit but right now I'm a *dad*.
A dad who loves his daughter and is desperate to see
her and she's not here and that completely
completely breaks me, every single bit, eating me up
with what I might've – all the wasted time of the last
few years and the thought that I might never –

A long moment.

NATALIE   So after you laughed at her what happened then?

Pause.

ANDY   That was pretty much it.

NATALIE   Had she finished what she was saying?

ANDY   She didn't have any more to say.

NATALIE   You mean she stopped talking after you laughed
at her.

ANDY   I didn't 'laugh at her'.

NATALIE   How would you put it?

ANDY

NATALIE   She stopped talking, but why do you think that
meant she didn't have anything else to say?

ANDY   Because she didn't say anything else.

NATALIE   Had you ever laughed at her before?

ANDY   Don't… you're making it sound like –

NATALIE   You don't like 'laughing at her' how would you describe it?

ANDY   Laughing with her.

NATALIE   Was she laughing?

ANDY   No I didn't laugh at her before.

NATALIE   You're sure?

ANDY   We had that kind of relationship, like, between us, we used to joke, make fun of each other but –

NATALIE   You made fun of her.

ANDY   We *made fun of each other*.

NATALIE   How did she make fun of you?

ANDY   Well she... she'd find me funny.

NATALIE   That's not / the same.

ANDY   When I teased her she'd laugh at it.

NATALIE   Would you say she was polite?

ANDY   Yes.

NATALIE   And she loved you?

          Beat.

ANDY   We had a good relationship.

NATALIE   How much did you speak to each other after that moment you laughed at her.

ANDY   We... we just both went to bed that night, I had to be up for work in the morning. No we didn't really... that was it.

NATALIE   Right.

          Okay then.

          Beat.

ANDY   So that's your theory. You think that's why she left for *two years*? Because I *laughed*?

He smiles.

Okay. I mean. Wow. Okay. That was all it took for. That I... okay.

He smiles again.

NATALIE   And this is why she would be right not to come back.

ANDY   What?

NATALIE   Because you're laughing at her again. Now.

ANDY   I'm not laughing *at her*

NATALIE   You are –

ANDY   I'm laughing at –

NATALIE   What else are you laughing at.

ANDY   You! It was a *discussion* we were having a heated discussion about our different views and as part of that part of the argument I might have laughed I might have done that but surely I've brought up an empowered, strong enough –

NATALIE   It's not about being strong –

ANDY   Young woman that she can answer back that she can take a laugh or just tell me to fuck off or whatever / if she's offended call –

NATALIE   Maybe she / doesn't want to have to tell you to fuck off

ANDY   – me out on it ask me *why* I'm laughing *ask me* if I don't respect her, not just keep that to herself how offended she was and then suddenly the next day text me to say she's left and not speak to me for *two years* come on come on Natalie you don't think that's an overreaction?

NATALIE   Look if this equation doesn't add up to you then you're missing a factor right and I'd say it's about

time to work out what that is. You had the
conversation with the laughing. She reacted in the
way you described. That is a fact yes –

ANDY   Well I think you're twisting –

NATALIE   No no listen to me for once, just / listen to what
I'm saying –

ANDY   For once? I've been mostly listening Natalie –

Beat. As she waits for him to stop talking over her.

NATALIE   She reacted as you yourself described so a few
things might be true:

Firstly, maybe she's weak, she can't deal with the
joke or the argument or answer back or all the
things you just said so she's not a strong person
she's a flakey representative of an overly sensitive
generation okay yeah maybe that's it.

ANDY   No, I'm not saying that, and that's not / her at all –

NATALIE   Or perhaps when it happened it tapped into
something bigger, that had been going on a long
time, and in that moment she saw in you something
that she couldn't handle any more, that this wasn't
the only time something like this had happened
maybe this was just the most acute and hurtful
instance of it. That for some reason you didn't
respect her at all, and you treated her like a child

ANDY   She was a child.

NATALIE   She was not.

ANDY   *My child* –

NATALIE   and I bet –

ANDY   She'll *always* / be my child –

NATALIE   just a *hunch* that she would *never* have laughed at
you and your position and what you were saying
that actually she was interested why you voted that

way and knew there were legitimate reasons she didn't think you were a racist or stupid she really wanted to know but for some reason when she said it the other way you were laughing in her face and she realised you often did that and that there was nothing she could say or do that would stop it.

ANDY / You don't know.

NATALIE There was no respect, or recognition of her as a real person, the mocking the sarcasm the pigeonholing and reducing and laughing, so characteristic of you and your world and your laddy easy-banter generation would carry on unless she –

ANDY / *You don't know.*

NATALIE – turned round and got out of there and now she has I wonder if actually she's developed as a person I wonder if she's discovered who she really is, and embraced all the strange things that make her different if maybe she has thrived.

Pause.

ANDY Why does this matter to you?

But she's very emotional. He can see it. She's let her guard down.

NATALIE All I'm saying is. I suppose. If you want her to come in the door. If you want to *maximise* the chances of that, you might want to call her up now, and leave a message telling her that you think you've figured out what it was. What you did. And that you're sorry. And that –

ANDY Sorry that I laughed?

NATALIE (interrupting again) Yes.

ANDY But... I'm... That's simply normal human interaction. If we say I can't do that then you're policing behaviour so tightly we might as well – it's Orwellian.

NATALIE   'Orwellian.'

ANDY   Yes.

NATALIE   You laughed at your daughter in her face when
           she was telling you something of vital importance /
           I don't think it's –

ANDY   You're saying the Brexit vote was of 'vital
           importance'?

NATALIE   Yes. Why? Wasn't it to you?

ANDY   She was completely free to laugh at me back.

NATALIE   I'm guessing that's not her style. You need to break
           all this stuff apart. Cos all this stuff, it's gone.
           Boot-cut jeans. *X-Files*. CDs. Nokia phones.
           Ladettes. Spice Girls. *NME*. Cool Brittania. Blair
           was a criminal. Saville was a paedo. Morrissey's
           basically always been a racist. I know that's
           everything you grew up with but most of it is very
           offensive and it's now, quite rightly been burnt to
           the ground.

ANDY   Why are you being so unkind?

NATALIE   I'm... what?

ANDY   You can see how upsetting this is for me right?

NATALIE   You want me to take responsibility for your
           feelings?

ANDY   No I want you to stop being unkind.

NATALIE   I'm... I don't think I am. Being unkind. I... just...

           A moment. NATALIE*'s upset too.*

           I just think you're not being fair to her.

ANDY   And that matters to you why?

           Beat.

           You want another cup of tea?

NATALIE   She might be here any minute.

ANDY   Yes but you're shaking.

NATALIE   What?! I'm not... Shaking?!

ANDY   Okay fine but do you want a cup of tea?

NATALIE   Yeah. Okay. Thanks.

            He goes through into the kitchen.

            A moment. Then she calls through to him.

            I'm just trying to say to you that if there's a chance
            it's going to make a difference I don't see what
            possible reason you wouldn't try it, just call her
            and say sorry. It's not Orwellian it's just civilised
            behaviour I mean how can it be a bad thing to hold
            yourself to a higher standard and if you got it
            wrong to say sorry. Why is that a problem?

            But – you know – Up to you.

            Now he's out of the room, NATALIE *gets out her
            phone and texts.*

            She finishes. Sends it.

            A moment.

            Then ANDY *comes back in with two more cups of
            tea. He gives her one.*

            Thanks. I might just...

            He then goes to his phone. Picks it up.

            Dials MAYA's *number.*

            What are you doing?

ANDY   Calling her. I think you're right.

NATALIE   Really?

ANDY   Yeah.

NATALIE   You making a point or something?

ANDY   No you persuaded me.

NATALIE   Oh. Oh right. Oh. I wasn't expecting that.

It rings then – it's answered.

ANDY   She... She's...

On the phone.

Hello?

No answer.

Hello?

(*To* NATALIE.) Someone's answered.

Back to the phone.

Maya? It's Dad.

He turns away.

Maya?

Maya, if you're there, I really want you back, for Christmas. We can talk. Sort everything out.

– and I... I know now, I think, why you went. Maybe I'm wrong, but I promise if you want to come and talk, I won't laugh at you. Like I did the day before you left.

If it is that, that upset you, then I'm... sorry. It wasn't my intention and if you want to come I promise I'll be careful. I won't be rude.

I just... I really miss you Maya. I miss you. Come and see me, in the hall tonight, and we can try to... to...

Are you there?

The phone goes dead.

Maya. Maya?

He stops.

A moment of silence.

NATALIE   I thought that was good. What you said.

ANDY   You wanted me to call.

You were so keen.

Beat.

Did you know she would answer?

How could you know?

A sound at the door. Just outside.

NATALIE   It's a dragon.

ANDY   What?

NATALIE   Her tattoo. A dragon with wings.

A moment. The outside door opens.

MAYA *enters.*

ANDY   Oh.

He's unsure what to do.

Hi.

A moment. They look at each other.

Blackout.

End of Act Two.

ACT THREE

As we left it.

ANDY *takes a step towards* MAYA. *Then stops.*

ANDY   Come in.

          She comes a little further into the room.

          You got my message.

MAYA   Yeah.

          Looks at them.

ANDY   And you. You're...

MAYA   We're together yeah.

ANDY   Together. Okay.

MAYA   I didn't want to come in till I knew how you were. What you were feeling.

ANDY   Okay. So you... you sent her in, instead.

NATALIE   She didn't send me. I suggested it.

ANDY   To test me.

MAYA   To talk to you. To find out how you were. It's a big thing.

ANDY   Right. So all the stuff she was saying was...

          Right.

          Beat.

          I had this whole plan of what I'd do when you arrived. But it... it doesn't matter now does it. Can I get you anything? A cup of tea? Hot chocolate? Sorry about all this. Especially with it not working. There's supposed to be lights and... stuff... It's stupid.

MAYA   It's not.

ANDY   I thought when I threw out the decorations, threw
            out all our scenes, after Mum died, I thought maybe
            that was why you'd gone. Not the only reason but –

            That's why I wanted to do this. But it doesn't work.

            Anyway, I'm pleased you're back.

            He turns to NATALIE.

            So you're not from round here at all.

NATALIE   No.

ANDY   You don't know Gilly.

NATALIE   Maya told me about Gilly. We met at university.
            I'm from London.

ANDY   London right, and you two –

NATALIE   We're staying in an Airbnb in Kiddylington.

MAYA   Kidlington.

NATALIE   Kidlington.

ANDY   Right.

MAYA   This is strange.

ANDY   Yeah it is.

            ANDY *looks at her. Then turns to* NATALIE.

            You don't actually need any of this stuff then?
            The plates?

NATALIE   Maya was worried if she came and spoke to you
            herself it would be the same as it was. She
            wouldn't do it. So I said okay well why don't I talk
            to you first, which she agreed to, but we had a
            sense that if I'd told you who I was, there's no way
            you'd have listened.

            So no I don't need the plates. But a lot of what
            I said was true. My mum is mad and has twenty
            people round for Christmas each year.

And whatever I said it got you both in the same room.

Beat. ANDY *turns to* MAYA.

ANDY   Do you want to sit down?

MAYA   Yeah. Sure.

ANDY   Yeah let's sit down. Let's all...

They move some chairs to sit down – as they do, quietly –

NATALIE Maybe I should –

MAYA   No.

NATALIE *stays and they sit.*

ANDY   You look older.

In a good way.

Your hair's different.

And you look happy. You seem happy.

MAYA   Yeah. We are.

ANDY   How long have you been together?

MAYA   Six months.

ANDY   Cool.

That 'cool' is left to hang in the air. Not a word he's ever used before really.

And is Natalie your... I mean when you left you were with, you were dating boys.

MAYA   Natalie's my first serious girlfriend yeah.

ANDY   Right.

MAYA   My first serious anything actually.

ANDY   Yeah.

Well.

You've done alright.

MAYA   Er... okay.

ANDY   I mean she's very articulate clearly.

MAYA   Did she talk a lot?

ANDY   Just a little bit.

NATALIE   We both talked a lot.

            A moment.

MAYA   So who was it that saw us together? In the café?

ANDY   Julie.

MAYA   Right.

ANDY   With the neck?

MAYA   Yeah yeah. I didn't see her. We came about a week
            ago, so Natalie had a sense of it. I wanted to show
            her around, so she knew what she was getting in to.

            Beat. ANDY *might cry. And he doesn't want to.*

ANDY   You want a mince pie?

MAYA   Sure.

NATALIE   I'll get them.

ANDY   No. No it's okay.

            He goes off to the kitchen to get them.

MAYA   How was it?

NATALIE   Yeah.

            He's actually trying really hard.

MAYA   What?

NATALIE   Just – I think he gets it.

MAYA   Okay but I'm telling you, after a while –

NATALIE   I think he really wants to do / what it takes to –

MAYA   You've known him twenty minutes. You said he
            sounded toxic and I should move on.

NATALIE   Yeah from what you told me –

MAYA   And that's true. I can't spend my life –

NATALIE   He called you and apologised. We didn't –

MAYA   Only just. Look we agreed what would happen, I'll say what I need to say, then we can –

ANDY *comes back in from the kitchen with the packet of mince pies.*

ANDY   Couldn't get the oven working. Must be on the same power ring as the sockets. But we can have them cold, won't matter will it?

He takes one out. Give it to MAYA. *One to* NATALIE.

Couldn't find any plates.

NATALIE   We just packed them.

ANDY   Oh. Yeah. Course.

MAYA   Thanks.

He smiles. Sits. Eats the mince pie a bit.

A moment.

ANDY   Can I ask a question?

MAYA   Sure.

ANDY   I understand why you left. I get that now. That maybe I didn't respect you. Laughed at you. All the banter whatever. For a while. For years. You needed some space from that. I don't...

No well I get that.

But I don't understand why you've come back.

I mean I'm pleased you have. More than. It's amazing to –

But… You're clearly, I mean I don't know, but you seem –

Beat.

I just heard you talking. Not exactly what you said but…

Toxic?

Beat.

So why have you come back?

MAYA *and* NATALIE *look at each other.*

MAYA   I always used to complain about you. To Nat. And she… one day, she said what are you going do about it then? And I said there's nothing I can do about it. And she said she thought I should talk to you. Say the things to you that I'd be saying to her.

ANDY   Okay.

MAYA   And then there was this one specific thing. That happened.

ANDY   What?

          Beat.

MAYA   You want to know?

ANDY   Of course.

MAYA   Okay.

          Alright. So I'm at Leeds. University. We both are. I'm doing Philosophy and English.

ANDY   Wow.

NATALIE   History of Art.

ANDY   Sure.

MAYA   Yeah, and I'm good there. Mates. Natalie. Got a job.

ANDY   Good.

MAYA   Yeah but then… so one day we heard the Prime
            Minister was visiting the university? She was
            opening some new wing? The science wing I think.
            And a bunch of us were talking about how we
            should try and speak to her. Lots of people are going
            to protest and we'll do that, but we thought we
            should actually try and have a conversation with her.

ANDY   You mean speak to her.

MAYA   Yeah but –

ANDY   Wow, okay.

MAYA   but it would only be like –

ANDY   Good luck.

MAYA   – only be a few words before someone stopped us
            but it would be worth it. So we found out that she
            was touring the new building, then walking with
            the vice-chancellor across to the Great Hall to
            speak to selected people. And we thought if we
            could get in the hall early that day, maybe we could
            wait, then come out and get to her. So three of us
            agreed we would. Me, Steve, and Biscuit.

ANDY   Biscuit.

MAYA   It's what she's called by everyone. It was her first
            word as a toddler, so –

ANDY   What about Natalie?

MAYA   I… I didn't tell Natalie.

ANDY   Why not?

            Beat.

NATALIE   I'd have told her not to do it.

MAYA   It's important.

NATALIE   Yeah I know but –

ANDY   – but you're trying to get to the Prime Minister and
            you might be shot.

NATALIE   Exactly.

MAYA   Yeah anyway so the day comes and we've got a
            friend who's involved and we get in, help with the
            chairs then we go along the corridor, and no one
            stops us. They let us go past. Then we see her,
            Theresa, walking out of the science block – about
            to walk past the protesters and we're there, on the
            inside of the barriers, and no one's noticed us.
            She's getting closer, talking to students who are the
            head of the union and have done well, whatever,
            and we're now at the end of that line. And you
            realise yeah, when she's this close up, what a
            performance it all is?

ANDY   Of course.

MAYA   The way she stands, how she holds her head, it's so
            deliberate. Makes everyone sort of shrink. She
            shakes someone's hand and they fucking curtsy,
            and she's nearly at us, and I look at Biscuit and
            Steve, to work out who's going to start and they've
            taken a step back. Not a huge step but they've
            edged their way out of this line and towards the
            barrier. Away from her.

ANDY   Right.

MAYA   With the armed police, and the vice-chancellor and
            all the rest, they're not going to take the risk, and
            I realise in that moment that all the stuff we've
            spoken about in the pub for nights and nights and
            months, the need for revolution, for REAL change,
            for patriarchy to be dismantled, for the country to be
            fair, for capitalism to be destroyed, they don't want
            that. They want to be liked, and approved of, and
            they want it all to stay the same. Despite knowing
            that doing that, defying the establishment is the only
            way genuine progress occurs. The founding fathers,

the independence movement from empire, the sixties, gay rights, Apartheid – they all needed to have genuine passion, defiance, destruction and a total lack of deference. And I realise that it turns out, between all these hundreds of people, there's only one, today, who genuinely believes she has a duty to speak truth to power. I'm the only fucking one. You know what I mean?

ANDY   Sure.

MAYA   So now's the moment. Do I believe the shit I've been talking or do I not? But before I can answer that, she's there, Theresa, and I'll be fucked if I'm not going to say what I think.

I say Prime Minister? And she turns, smiles, puts her hand out. Says Hello. I shake her hand and say hello. Can I ask you a couple of questions? And she says well I don't know if… but I carry on –

And as I do, I realise there's so many cameras on me, so many eyes looking at me now. Like hundreds of camera phones, lots of actual cameras, and the whole crowd from the protesters to the vice-chancellor, all wondering who this weird girl is.

And I say Prime Minister do you have any idea of what you've done to this country to almost every aspect of it, from the policies of austerity that you were all warned would result in thousands of deaths to Windrush to Universal Credit – …

She's looking at me intently and I'm talking but then…

…my stomach is doing this weird thing of convulsing, and stopping me speaking and I can feel my lip tensing in the way that it does when I'm going to cry, and my voice has gone, and my face is red, and she steps forward and she says, this woman, this Anti-fucking-Christ robot woman says

'Are you okay? Are you alright?'

She puts a hand on me, she puts her Tory right
hand on my pure left arm. I pull it away. I turn and
go, run away before anyone can –

And get back to my room, don't want to see
anyone because I know that I'll be on the news, on
social media, everywhere for ever the little girl
who tried to take on the Prime Minister but was
such a fucking… snowflake that she couldn't finish
a sentence without bursting into tears and she, that
right-wing robot dancing thing will get points from
the fact she was compassionate 'are you okay' –
and that is basically my life over.

I don't look at anything for an hour. Then I check
my phone and… There's nothing. Just a text from
Biscuit apologising.

I go onto the news websites. Look for coverage of
the event. I search Twitter. There's nothing.

I thought they were all over it, but I suppose I didn't
actually say anything so it wasn't… of interest.

I'm lucky. But I know where it came from. That…
shaking. That thing that happened in me that
stopped me talking. It's the panic that –

ANDY   Yeah I understand.

MAYA   Of not being listened to, of being dismissed,
            laughed at and it's what she's been saying for
            a long time, that I need to say these things to you,
            whether you'll hear them or not.

ANDY   I am. I'm listening.

            Beat.

            That's amazing. That you wanted to confront her.

MAYA   Yeah but the point is that I couldn't. I ran away
            from you but you're still there in my head.

ANDY

MAYA   …

ANDY

MAYA   There are other things I've been thinking. That
            I need to say. Because I did things wrong too.

            Like I'm sorry about the way I went. And for not
            contacting you. I think after everything that was
            going on, I needed to get out, I think that was the
            right decision for me, but I didn't need to do it like
            that, I know you must've been worried.

ANDY   Yeah well. Yes I was.

MAYA   And I know I wasn't always good to you. When
            Mum died I was horrible to you, a lot. For quite
            a while.

ANDY   Oh but that was –

MAYA   I know you must've been so… devastated too
            and –

ANDY   You were fifteen.

MAYA   Yeah but even so –

ANDY   You were a child.

MAYA   Well not / completely –

ANDY   I didn't mind at all. I understood that.

            Beat.

MAYA   Okay. It's just when I thought about it –

ANDY   No.

MAYA   I think that was why –

ANDY   It wasn't –

MAYA   – why you lost respect for me because –

ANDY   That was / why I lost…?

MAYA   – because when I got frustrated /

ANDY   Maya honestly / that's enough –

MAYA   I used to be quite cruel and I want / to say
            something clearly to you about it, I think it's
            important that you hear them so –

ANDY   Cruel? No no not true you thought I lost respect for
            you because you were calling me names?! Come
            on Maya!

            He laughs. Pause.

            You were a teenager, you'd lost your mum, I mean
            that's / big. You had no way –

MAYA   *You're doing it now you're doing it again you're
            laughing.*

            He stops. Stares at them.

            The smile gone suddenly. He stares at them.

            A moment.

            Then he looks down at his mince pie.

ANDY   Sorry.

            You were –

            He starts to cry. It's awkward.

            MAYA *sits. Neither her or* NATALIE *knows what
            to do.*

            I'm trying.

            A moment.

            NATALIE *stands up.*

NATALIE   Excuse me.

            She goes out.

            He sucks up the crying. Looks up at MAYA.

ANDY   Keep going. Say what you were going to say.
            If you want.

MAYA   I was cruel to you when it all happened. And I'm sorry for that. But yes, I was fifteen, and I don't think you should have taken it so personally and treated me the way you did. You stopped being kind to me after that.

You asked why I came here. Why we did all this.

I'm sorry if you thought it's because I'm... going to stay.

I'm not.

I wanted to say all this stuff, say sorry for the things I'd done wrong, and I wanted you to know the truth about why I can't be here any more.

Suddenly the fairy lights around the hall and the tree come on.

The CD player starts up and is playing Magdalen College Choir – 'In the Bleak Midwinter'.

NATALIE *enters – she's found the fuse board.*

NATALIE   Hey!

MAYA   What?

NATALIE   Found the switch in the kitchen. Sorry to interrupt. Wait a minute.

She switches off the main lights in the hall, then reaches over and switches on the Christmas scene. The lights in the house come on. Snow falls on it. The figure on the pond starts skating. The scene is complete.

Magic!

MAYA *looks at it, in detail.* ANDY *stands back.*

It's beautiful.

ANDY   Maybe... Just tomorrow, come over, spend Christmas with me, and see. Both of you. And if after that, you do want to say goodbye and go for ever then… fair enough.

NATALIE   I know this might sound strange but I've spent some time with your dad and because if we don't think people can change we're totally screwed aren't we, and he has apologised and he is doing his best, and he made me a cup of tea, which I wasn't expecting. Before we came in I know we were like 'he needs the truth' and 'he needs to understand' but I really think he does now, and my mum's mad, you don't think she needs a bit of work too? I'm being romantic, but all I can say is if it was me, and it's not I know, but if it was, I'd give him a chance.

It's totally up to you.

And at the very least this is awesome.

MAYA *looks at the scene. She's crying.*

MAYA   It's our house. The pond.

Is that – skating – is that…?

ANDY   That's you.

MAYA   And at the door – you're watching.

So this is…

Where's Mum?

ANDY   Mum's not there. It's not the past Maya.

I know that's gone.

This is what I'm after.

At least once a year.

(*To* NATALIE.) Sorry, I didn't know about you.

NATALIE   Yeah no worries.

ANDY   I can add you in.

NATALIE   Okay.

    ANDY turns back to MAYA.

ANDY   Can we not at least… try?

    A long moment.

    MAYA holds NATALIE's hand.

    Looks at ANDY.

MAYA   What time tomorrow?

ANDY   Ten.

    Beat.

MAYA   Okay.

ANDY   Thank you.

    A moment.

NATALIE   Happy Christmas.

    She kisses MAYA.

MAYA   Yeah.

    MAYA turns to her father.

    Happy Christmas Dad.

    Beat.

ANDY   Happy Christmas.

    Music continues and we fade to blackout.

    End.

A Nick Hern Book

Snowflake first published in Great Britain in 2018 as a paperback original by Nick Hern Books Limited, The Glasshouse, 49a Goldhawk Road, London W12 8QP, in association with the Old Fire Station

Snowflake copyright © 2018 Mike Bartlett

Mike Bartlett has asserted his right to be identified as the author of this work

Cover design by Rebecca Pitt

Designed and typeset by Nick Hern Books, London
Printed in Great Britain by Mimeo Ltd, Huntingdon, Cambridgeshire PE29 6XX

A CIP catalogue record for this book is available from the British Library

ISBN 978 1 84842 817 1

Woodland
CARBON
www.woodlandcarbon.co.uk
NICK HERN BOOKS
Printed on Carbon Captured paper